Michael Pellowski's
LUNCHROOM LAUGHS JOKE BOOK

D1291999

DARBY CREEK PUBLISHING

~ To Audrey & Howard Snyder ~

Copyright © 2005 by Darby Creek Publishing

Cover illustration by John Pound
Interior illustrations by Tim Davis

Cataloging-in-Publication

Pellowski, Michael..
Michael Pellowski's lunchroom laughs joke book / cover art by John Pound;
interior art by Tim Davis.
          p. ; cm.
ISBN-13: 978-1-58196-032-8
ISBN-10: 1-58196-032-8
Summary: Here are some snappy jokes and riddles for you and your friends to
share over lunch at school.
1. Food—Humor. 2. School lunchrooms, cafeterias, etc.—Humor. 3. Wit and
humor, Juvenile. [1. Food—Humor. 2. School lunchrooms, cafeterias, etc.—
Humor. 3. Jokes.] I. Title. II. Alt. title. III. III. IV. III.
PN6231.F66 P43 2005
[818/.5402] dc22
OCLC: 57425957

Published by Darby Creek Publishing
7858 Industrial Parkway
Plain City, OH 43064
www.darbycreekpublishing.com

Printed in the United States of America

2 4 6 8 10 9 7 5 3 1

1-58196-032-8

Michael Pellowski's
Lunchroom Laughs Joke Book

cover art by
John Pound

interior art by
Tim Davis

TABLE OF

CONTENTS

LOONY LUNCH TIME

How was lunch?

Mr. Baseball Player:
"I cleaned my plate!"

Mr. Turkey:
"I gobbled it up!"

Mr. Ham:
"I made a pig of myself!"

Mr. Feather:
"I chowed 'down'!"

Mr. Fish:
"I wasn't very hungry, so I just nibbled."

Mr. Hole:
"It filled me up."

....

Student: Hey! My taco is cold.

Cook: Here! Put some
          hot sauce on it.

Matt: Why are you bringing a pair
of scissors into the cafeteria?

Pat: I want to cut in the lunch line.

....

Cook: Our students have rude
eating habits.

Principal: I'll ask them to be neater
and more mannerly at lunch.
What are you making today?

Cook: Sloppy Joes.

....

What do you get when you
cross a hen, a French dog,
and warm broth?

Chicken poodle soup!

Show Time!

Show me a person who brings a jump rope to the cafeteria—and I'll show you someone who plans to skip lunch!

....

Sal: I used to eat my lunch
       during math class.

Hal: Why did you stop?

Sal: I was becoming a problem eater.

....

Cook: I served 10,000 beef
             hamburgers for lunch
             yesterday.

Principal: Now that sounds like
             a lot of bull.

Daffy
Definitions

What do you call lunch gossip?

Dining rumors.

What do you call angel food cake?

A heavenly snack.

What do you call cinnamon rolls?

The Spice Curls.

....

Why does a *T* rex always
buy lunch at school?

*Because it's impossible to pack
a brontosaurus into a lunch box.*

Who is in charge of the
astronauts' cafeteria?

The launch lady.

....

What did the nice sandwich say
to the mean sandwich?

"Hey, pal! What's eating you?"

....

What do you get when you cross
a cafeteria lady with a teacher?

A cooking lesson!

....

Why did the girl bring a
lifeguard to the cafeteria?

*She needed someone to
help her save some seats.*

Hey! There's chicken for lunch today!

Egg-cellent!

Let's scramble to the cafeteria!

Oh, what a fowl meal!

You'd have to be a cluck to eat that!

I don't want to hear another peep about today's lunch.

· ·

Principal: Our lunchroom is so clean the students can eat off the floor.

Parent: Can't the school board afford tables?

Barry: These biscuits taste like dog bones.

Larry: I think the cook used "collie flour" to make them.

....

Alphabet Lunch Menu

Split-P soup

M & Ms candy

T-Bone steak

Spaghetti-Os

C-food

Iced-T

D-zert

Why did Dracula run into the lunchroom?

He only had time for a quick bite!

....

Mel: I paid ten bucks for this
     sandwich!

Nel: That's baloney!

Mel: No. It's roast beef.

....

Ted: Does your cafeteria make good
     hot dogs?

Ed: Frankly, the wieners are losers.

....

Student: Hey! Something's buzzing
           in my sandwich!

Cook: That's because it's a Bee-L-T!

Cook:	You're fortunate. We're giving away free lunches today.
Pupil:	What are you serving?
Cook:	Pot luck. Do you want some?
Pupil:	No, thanks. I won't chance eating it.

....

The Lunchroom's Silly Staff

Mrs. Bea Quiet
— *lunchroom aide*

Mr. Hal Sweep-up
— *custodian*

Ms. Selma Food
— *cashier*

Mr. Kenny Cooke
— *school chef*

Parent: Why are the students eating in the dark?

Principal: Because the light bulbs went out for lunch.

. . . .

Parent: Do you allow grace in the lunchroom?

Principal: Of course we do.
Grace sits next to Hope and Melanie.

. . . .

SILLY SIGN ON A DOG:

Flea Lunch Here!

SNACK SNICKERS

Student: Weren't we supposed to have chili for lunch?

Cook: Yes. But it was a secret.

Student: So why aren't we having chili?

Cook: Someone spilled the beans.

....

How do you make a football hero sandwich?

Use All-American cheese.

....

How do you make a down-to-earth sandwich?

Use lots of "ground" beef.

....

What did the wide receiver say to the quarterback at the lunch table?

"Pass the salt!"

Ann: I never buy lunch at school. The cafeteria food is garbage.

Fran: So what do you eat for lunch?

Ann: I bring lots of junk food from home.

....

Nick: Take a bite of this sandwich. I made it myself. It's really good.

Rick: You don't expect me to swallow that, do you?

....

Teacher: What do you want to drink with your lunch?

Cheerleader: Root beer!

....

Boy: You stole my milk money!

Bully: That's udder nonsense!

Eddie: Why are you eating that
          five dollar bill?

Freddie: It's my lunch money.

....

Mike: Why does the man in charge
          of our school eat such a huge
          lunch?

Spike: It's his principal meal of
          the day.

....

Boy: Why are you fixing your hair
          at the lunch table?

Girl: I always brush after every
          meal.

22

What does a perfectionist eat
for lunch?

Neatloaf.

....

How do you fix a broken
lasagna dish?

Use tomato paste!

....

Teacher: I'm going to go jogging during
my lunch period.

Cook: Why don't you just eat on
the run?

....

Cook: The lunches I make stick to
your ribs.

Student: I know. But who likes to eat
paste?

Teacher: How long do you bake
          your macaroni and cheese?

Cook: Until it's perfectly golden
          brown on top or until
          the fire alarm goes off.

....

Cook: We're having spy burgers
          for lunch.

Principal: What are they made of?

Cook: I can't tell you. It's a
          secret recipe.

....

Phil: Who sits at that lunch table?

Lil: The cheerleading squad.

Phil: Humph! It's no wonder that
          table has so many chairs
          (cheers).

What sport can you play
in the lunchroom?

Picnic basket ball.

....

How do golfers stay healthy?

They eat lots of greens for lunch.

....

What do you feed an angel for lunch?

Soul food.

....

Which vegetable was a villain
in *Star Wars*?

Darth Tater.

DON'T KNOCK THE FOOD

Knock! Knock!

Who's there?

Rye.

Rye who?

Rye did you eat my snack cake?

···

Knock! Knock!

Who's there?

Lime.

Lime who?

Lime in love with
our substitute teacher.

Knock! Knock!

Who's there?

Swish.

Swish who?

Swish cheese has holes in it.

....

Knock! Knock!

Who's there?

Taco.

Taco who?

Taco the time you need
to eat your lunch.

Knock! Knock!

Who's there?

Wheat.

Wheat who?

Wheat like to eat lunch
at your table.

• •

Knock! Knock!

Who's there?

Tuna.

Tuna who?

Tuna your instrument
before music class starts.

Knock! Knock!

Who's there?

Cracker.

Cracker who?

Cracker up by telling her
a good joke at lunch!

....

Knock! Knock!

Who's there?

Thermos.

Thermos who?

Thermos be a better place
to eat than the school cafeteria.

Knock! Knock!

Who's there?

Dewey.

Dewey who?

Dewey have to eat
this junk for lunch?

....

Knock! Knock!

Who's there?

Pastry.

Pastry who?

Pastry blocks in the three
empty squares.

Knock! Knock!

Who's there?

Gravy.

Gravy who?

Gravy, Gravy Crockett,
King of the Wild Frontier.

....

Knock! Knock!

Who's there?

Veal.

Veal who?

Veal get together after lunch.

Knock! Knock!

Who's there?

Chicken.

Chicken who?

Chicken tests is what teachers
do at home.

•••

Knock! Knock!

Who's there?

Ice cream.

Ice cream who?

Ice cream every time
I watch a scary movie.

Knock! Knock!

Who's there?

Ketchup.

Ketchup who?

Ketchup on your homework
or you'll fail this class.

....

Knock! Knock!

Who's there?

Butternut.

Butternut who?

Butternut be late again
or I'll give you detention.

Knock! Knock!

Who's there?

Juicy.

Juicy who?

Juicy what they're serving
for lunch today? YUCK!

....

Knock! Knock!

Who's there?

Pudding.

Pudding who?

Pudding your lunch money
in a safe place is a good idea.

Knock! Knock!

Who's there?

Soda.

Soda who?

Soda football team finally
won a game? Good for them!

....

Knock! Knock!

Who's there?

Doughnut.

Doughnut who?

Doughnut bother me
while I'm eating.

37

Knock! Knock!

Who's there?

Chili.

Chili who?

Chili weather is expected
in December.

....

Knock! Knock!

Who's there?

Menu.

Menu who?

Menu wish upon a star,
your dreams come true.

Knock! Knock!

Who's there?

V.

V who?

V vant pizza for lunch.

....

Knock! Knock!

Who's there?

Olive.

Olive who?

Olive to eat salami sandwiches.

THE MERRY MENU

A Timely Lunch Menu

Minute steak

Minute rice

Two-minute eggs

Instant pudding

....

What is Frosty the Snowman's
favorite part of the cake?

The icing.

....

Cara: My dog likes Chinese food.

Lara: Maybe he's a chow-chow mein.

What villain from *Star Wars*
is covered with tomato sauce
and cheese?

Jabba the Pizza Hut!

....

What did Frosty have for dessert?

A snow cone.

What kind of breakfast cereal
does Frosty eat for lunch?

Sugar-frosted snowflakes.

....

Grouchy Teacher: Grr—I hate having
fish sticks for lunch
every Friday.

Cook: Okay. Next Friday I'll serve
something that will suit you
better. How about crabcakes?

The Geography Lunch Menu

A California burger

Philadelphia cream cheese

Boston cream pie

New England clam chowder

Kentucky fried chicken

Idaho potatoes

Washington apples

Boston baked beans

New York strip steak

Texas toast

Mr. Bologna: I feel sick.

Mr. Salami: You should be home
              in bread.

....

How do you make lunch
for a robber?

Look up a recipe in a crook book!

....

What famous writer makes
a great sandwich?

Sir Francis Bacon-Lettuce-and-Tomato.

....

What did the golfer eat for lunch?

A sub-par sandwich.

What kind of soup did
the art teacher have for lunch?

Doodle soup.

....

Jenny: Why do you have alphabet
         soup for lunch every day?

Denny: It's a meal that's
         letter perfect.

....

John: How long will it take you
        to eat that minute steak?

Lon: About sixty seconds.

Chester: This is my famous locomotive sandwich.

Lester: Why do you call it that?

Chester: Because sometimes I bite off more than I can chew! chew!

....

Marty: What do you call these tiny salted potato snacks?

Artie: Micro-chips.

....

What is the best kind of soup to eat before an exam?

Cram chowder!

....

What did the math teacher eat for dessert?

Pi (π) à la mode.

Teacher: George! You have food all over your face. Didn't you use a napkin at lunch?

George: Yes, teacher. I blew my nose in it.

....

Cafeteria Lady: Would you like some buttered buns?

Gym Teacher: No. I'd rather have some forward rolls.

....

What did the spider eat for dessert?

Webbing cake.

....

Cafeteria Lady: Do you have time for lunch, Mr. Fisherman?

Mr. Fisherman: No. I'll catch a bite later.

Don: I don't like having
lamb stew for lunch.

Ron: Why not?

Don: It leaves a "baa" taste
in my mouth.

....

What did Billy Shakespeare
have for lunch?

A Ham-let sandwich.

....

What do you get if you cross a bad
joke with a hamburger?

A corny beef sandwich.

....

Principal: Why did you get a job
cooking hamburgers
in the cafeteria?

Cook: I wanted to "meat"
new friends.

Jungle Lunch

Three hungry lions were first in line at the jungle lunchroom. The cafeteria door was closed while the cooks prepared the food.

Suddenly, a pushy zebra cut in front of the lions. Then a wiseguy antelope sneaked in behind the zebra.

Finally, a nasty hippo wedged his way in the line between the antelopes and the lions.

The zebra, the antelope, and the hippo all laughed as the angry lions grumbled about the animals cutting in line.

Minutes later, the cafeteria door opened and the three lions were first in line again.

"Come in," invited the lunchroom aide. "We're ready to serve lunch."

The first two lions burped. "No, thanks," said the third lion as he and his friends walked away patting their tummies. "We've already eaten."

Betty: What's that rabbit doing in the school cafeteria?

Eddie: He heard we were having "hoppy" meals for lunch.

....

Student: The school menu says we're having caveman food today.

Cook: That's right. I'm serving club sandwiches.

....

What's the best thing to feed the track team before a meet?

Fast food.

....

What does a sprinter drink with his lunch?

Running water.

What did the basketball team
eat for lunch?

Jumping beans and "swish" cheese.

....

Why did Mr. Watch go back
into the lunch line?

He wanted a "second" helping!

....

How did the plate get a crack in it?

It had a lunch break.

....

Jill: Why is your sandwich making
       sounds like car horns honking?

Bill: It's a peanut butter and
       traffic jam sandwich.

Barry: What do you have
for lunch?

Larry: A fish sandwich.
Do you want a taste?

Barry: Okay, I'll bite.

....

What's the best way to
serve a pigosaurus?

Make Jurassic Pork chops out of it.

....

What does the Green Giant
use to hold up his pants?

The Corn Belt.

....

Is the Green Giant smart?

No. He's a pea brain.

What did the Green Giant
say to the detective?

"Watch your peas and clues."

....

What kind of a pitch does the
Green Giant throw?

A bean ball.

....

Why do the Green Giant's feet ache?

He has corns on his toes.

....

What kind of nuts does the
Green Giant like?

Pea-nuts.

....

What did the carrots say
to the cabbage?

*"Stay out of the kitchen or you'll end up
in hot water."*

How can you make a bison fly?

Give him some buffalo wings.

....

Customer: I can't finish these frankfurters.

Waitress: I'll get you a hot doggie bag.

....

What is a beautician's favorite soft drink?

Dye-it soda.

....

What did the alphabet soup say to the noodle soup?

Let's go "bowl"ing together.

GAGGING ON THE FOOD

Seafood Special

What does a fencer like to eat?

Sword fish.

What does a cheap sailor like to eat?

A "sale"-fish.

What does a New Englander
like to eat?

A Cape Cod fish.

What does a salesman like to eat?

"Sell"-fish.

· ·

What does a beaver eat for lunch?

A "tree"-course meal!

Cook: The aroma of your new
        recipe is delightful.

Chef: Ah, the sweet smell
        of success.

....

Boy: I want two identical frozen
        milk desserts.

Lady: A couple of ice-cream clones
        coming right up.

....

Why did the farm boy feed
his cow peanuts?

*He wanted to have creamy-style
peanut butter for lunch!*

Spud Laffs

Mr. Fry: What happened to your potato car?

Mr. Spud: I mashed a fender.

....

How did Mr. Spud hit his golf ball out of the sand trap?

He used a potato wedge.

....

Mr. Fry: Is your potato car fast?

Mr. Spud: Yes. Watch it peel out.

....

Mr. Fry: How do you stop your potato car?

Mr. Spud: Don't you know how to "brake" a potato?

Show Time!

Show me a gold miner who
is a poultry cook—and I'll show
you a guy who makes great
chicken nuggets.

....

Where does a salsa crab live?

In a taco shell.

....

Knock! Knock!

Who's there?

Jamaica.

Jamaica who?

Jamaica good lunch today?

How about some alphabet soup?

It suits me to a **T**!

This meal has lots of **B** vitamins.

I like **C** food.

Feast your **I**s on this meal.

I like **P** soup better.

Can I have some Special **K** with it?

G, this is great.

O boy! I like it.

It's **E-Z** to prepare.

What does a detective put
on his hamburger?

Bar-b-clue sauce.

....

What did the squirrel say when he
saw what he was having for lunch?

"Ah, nuts!"

....

Knock! Knock!

Who's there?

Peas.

Peas who?

Peas don't talk with your mouth full.

How do you mail a slice of bread?

Take it to the toast office.

....

Boy: I'm a magician at lunch time.

Girl: What do you mean?

Boy: Put food in front of me and I'll make it disappear.

....

Girl: You've been making bad jokes since you stopped drinking your soda.

Boy: That's because I drank the "pun"-cola.

....

Jack: What is the choir having for lunch today?

Jill: Hymnburgers.

Daffy Definition

What do you call bad lemonade?

A bitter swill to swallow.

....

Sea Captain: I'm ready to eat my
sandwich for lunch.

Mate: Okay. I'll tell the cook
to bring up your sub.

....

Ned: Hurry up! Serve the food
already! Move it! Hurry up!

Ed: What's wrong with Ned?

Jed: When it comes to eating lunch,
he has a "wait" problem.

Food Advice

"Be tough,"
said Mr. Steak.

"Stick to it,"
said Mr. Oatmeal.

"Never lose your head,"
said Mr. Cabbage.

"Stick with your buds,"
said Mr. Potato.

"Make a lot of dough,"
said Mr. Pizza.

"Be sweet to everyone,"
said Ms. Sugarbeet.

"Have good taste,"
said Miss Spice.

Recipe for Success?

"Grow from the ground up,"
said Mr. Vegetable.

"Don't spread yourself too thin,"
said Mr. Butter.

"Branch out at the right times,"
said Mr. Stringbean.

"Keep your ears open,"
said Mr. Corn.

"Don't crack up under pressure,"
said Mr. Egg.

"Be thick-skinned,"
said Mr. Pineapple.

"Make a bunch of good friends,"
said Miss Grape.

T-Rex: Why do you like having
           dinosaur stew for lunch?

T-Rex, Jr.: Because you get such
           big portions.

....

What do you get when you
mix coffee with ham steaks?

Perk chops.

....

Which food ruled ancient Rome?

The Caesar salad.

....

Joe: Why are you wearing a clock
         on your stomach?

Moe: My doctor told me to "watch"
         my waistline.

Lester: How do you like the seafood I made for lunch today?

Chester: Are you fishing for a compliment?

....

Donnie: I made these shoes out of cooked ground beef.

Lonnie: Yuck! What do you call them, meat loafers?

....

Knock! Knock!

Who's there?

Raisin.

Raisin who?

Raisin my grades is tough.

Kerry: You eat like a bird.

Mary: Stop "pecking" on me.

···

What kind of pancakes
does an acrobat make?

Flipjacks.

···

How do you make vegetable jewelry?

*Put carrots (carats)
on an onion ring.*

···

Barry: Everyone in our lunch
group has a cold.

Gary: I know. We sit at a real
"coughy" table.

Dad: How was lunch today?

Son: Crumby.

Dad: Gee, that's too bad.

Son: No, it was great. I don't mind eating broken cookies for lunch.

....

Ginny: There's a bug on your lunch.

Minny: Yuck! I hate flyed chicken.

....

Knock! Knock!

Who's there?

Tea.

Tea who?

Tea you later, alligator!

73

Daffy
Definition

What do you call "mint"
chocolate chip ice cream?

A truly rich dessert.

....

Sara: Which girl in the lunchroom
is the richest kid in town?

Cara: See those girls walking
toward us?

Sara: Yes.

Cara: She's the one behind the butler
carrying a silver tray of food.

....

What do you get when a chef
sits on a hot stove?

A rump roasted.

Mr. Jones: My son has pet termites.
             He feeds them once a day.

Mr. Smith: So what's wrong with that?

Mr. Jones: They're eating me out of
             house and home.

....

John and Jack sat down to lunch.
When Jack opened his lunch box, it was
filled with thick, dark liquid.
   "What a stupid-looking lunch,"
John said. "Who made that slop?"
   "I did," Jack confessed, "and it wasn't
stupid-looking slop when I packed it
this morning. It started out as six
scoops of chocolate ice cream!"

....

Len: Did you swallow some
       feathers for lunch?

Ken: Yes. And I don't think
       I can keep them "down."

CHEWY CHUCKLES

What does a bee chew after lunch?

Buzzlegum.

....

What do you get when you
cross a hen house with hives?

Eggs over beesy.

....

What part of a pie does
a dentist like best?

The filling!

....

Principal: We had apples at lunch today.
Weren't we supposed to have
bananas?

Cook: Yes, I slipped up.

Knock! Knock!

Who's there?

Willow.

Willow who?

Willow be late for lunch
if we don't hurry.

· ·

Where did the millionaire
go after he ate his supper?

*To put his money in an
after-dinner mint.*

· ·

Boy: That diner is a bug-infested
restaurant.

Girl: I know. With every burger
you get free flies.

Lunch Laugh

Two farmers working in the fields got together at noon time because they wanted to have a "plower" lunch.

....

Knock! Knock!

Who's there?

Juicy.

Juicy who?

Juicy my lunch box? I lost it.

....

What do you get when you cross sardines with parakeets?

Fish and chirps.

Daffy Definition

What do you call a coffee break?

A job "perk."

....

What does a rabbit drink
on a cold day?

Hop chocolate.

....

What do you call a pig in blue pants?

Pork in jeans.

....

SILLY SIGN AT AN
AIR-CONDITIONED CAFETERIA:

We specialize in cold lunches.

What do you get when you cross
burgers and fries with toys?

Food that's fun to play with!

....

Principal: Do you ever make under-
cooked steaks for lunch?

Cook: On rare occasions.

....

Cook: I call this dish "alien stew."

Student: Why?

Cook: Because it's an Unidentified
          Fried Object.

....

What is a sheep's favorite soup?

Alphableat soup.

What does the abominable snowman eat for lunch?

Cold cuts

Frozen pizza

Chili dogs

Ice cream and snow cones

....

What do you put on the
windows of a vegetable jail?

Salad bars.

....

Who drinks soda and
is a savage fighter?

Colaman the Barbarian.

Knock! Knock!

Who's there?

Meal.

Meal who?

Meal see you after lunch, guys.

....

WANT AD

Cool cafeteria needs a hip chef:
Don't apply for the job
unless you really know
what's cooking.

....

What is the best side dish
to serve miners for lunch?

Coal slaw.

....

What do beavers eat with onion dip?

Wood chips.

Robin the Boy Wonder's Lunch

A super gyro

Alpha-"bat" soup

Hot wings

Batato salad

Hamburger batties

....

Which monk makes the
best French fries?

The Deep Friar Tuck.

....

What did the spud
say to the McIntosh?

"You're the apple of my eye."

Knock! Knock!

Who's there?

Jell-O.

Jell-O who?

Jell-O. Can your mom come
to the phone?

....

Jill: This is a ten-cent sandwich.

Bill: Why?

Jill: It's made with two slices of
      pumpernickel bread.

....

What kind of lunch does a vegetarian
make with two slices of bread?

A roast beet sandwich.

"Why are you wearing
roller blades in the cafeteria?"

*"I signed up for the
Meals-on-Wheels program."*

....

Knock! Knock!

Who's there?

Nut and honey.

Nut and honey who?

Nut and honey. I'm sorry
I interrupted you, dear.

....

What kind of birds do you
find in the cafeteria?

Swallows!

Girl: They say fish is brain food.

Boy: I eat fish three times a week.

Girl: So much for that theory.

....

Where do little goats eat their lunch?

At the kids' table.

....

What do you get when you
cross tuna with oatmeal?

Fish sticks to your ribs.

....

Student: I heard we're having roast owl
for lunch today?

Cook: Who? Who said that?

What's red and swims in the sea?

A strawberry jellyfish.

....

Knock! Knock!

Who's there?

Picnic.

Picnic who?

Picnic. He's the best player in school.

....

Rick: I crossed nuts with lemons and stuck it between two slices of bread.

Nick: What did it taste like?

Rick: A peanut bitter sandwich.

....

What's green, slender, and sour?

A toothpickle.

What do golfers drink with their lunch?

Iced tee.

....

Cara: White stuff dripped out of my
sandwich.

Lara: Now you have mayo knees.

....

How should you serve
lunch to a writer?

Use a paper plate!

....

Cafeteria aide: Why do you have a
pillow on your chair?

Student: I'm having a
sit-down meal.

....

Which holiday do vegetarians like best?

Crispmas Day.

Food Books

Detective Egg—
Its hero is a hard-boiled cop.

Ms. Spaghetti—
Its main character is a saucy gal.

The Licorice Mystery—
The plot has a lot of twists.

The Fishy Philosopher—
It's food for thought.

....

Knock! Knock!

Who's there?

Salad.

Salad who?

Salad to the highest bidder.

BROWN BAG BUFFOONERY

SCHOOL CAFETERIA

Principal: How did these double hamburgers get to the cafeteria?

Lunch lady: A big Mack truck delivered them.

....

What do you get when you cross Oreos with Frankenstein?

A cookie monster.

....

Ron: Should you knock on the cafeteria door if you want Mexican food for lunch?

Lon: No. Ring the Taco Bell.

Daffy Definition

What do you call nacho dip?

Salsa that belongs to someone else.

....

Knock! Knock!

Who's there?

Rye.

Rye who?

Rye do you keep asking me
all of these silly questions?

....

What does a *T* rex have for breakfast?

*Scrambled dinosaur eggs and
Jurassic Pork sausage.*

Art teacher: Why do you call your drawings Cheddar, Muenster, and Provolone?

Student: They're my cheese doodles.

....

What do you get when you cross an angry vegetable giant with a shark?

A *mean-green-eating-machine.*

....

Which fashion doll is like a spicy cookout?

Barbie-Q.

....

Ted: Why did you order turtle soup for lunch?

Jed: I like to eat slowly.

Anatomical
Lunch
Menu

Elbow macaroni

Heads of lettuce

Ears of corn

Crab legs

Prime rib

Chicken fingers

Rump roast

"Eyes" tea

Show Time!

Show me a bottle of
marshmallow soda pop—and I'll
show you a real soft drink.

....

What did one unripe lemon
say to the other?

"I hope you get bitter soon."

....

Why was the corn stalk crying?

It had a bad earache.

....

Which bug makes tasty pancakes?

Ant Jemima.

What does a lion eat with his soup?

Animal crackers.

....

What did the slice of bread
say to the margarine?

"Don't try to butter me up, pal."

....

Woman: What are those pastry
chefs doing?

Man: They're having a
pie-heating contest.

....

Student: Can I take this
pie-making class?

Cooking teacher: Sorry, the course
is filled.

Girl: Why are you sitting under the smoke alarm?

Boy: I'm eating five-alarm chili for lunch.

....

Cook: Do you want a cod fillet?

Pastor: No. I'm a sole man.

....

Boy: What kind of hamburger can I get for a dollar?

Cook: We're running a special today. You get four Quarter Pounders for a buck.

....

Benny: Watch me spell out an insult with my alphabet soup.

Lenny: Careful, pal, or I'll make you eat your words.

Daffy Definition

What do you call spare ribs?

A side order.

....

Bully: How would you like a knuckle
       sandwich for lunch?

Boy: No, thanks. I'm allergic
     to fist food.

....

Show Time!

Show me a lunch table directly under
an air-conditioning vent—and I'll show
you a table where the cool kids sit.

Ted: I came to lunch straight from wood shop.

Ed: Did you bring any table scraps with you?

....

Mr. Green: I teach a class on nuclear energy at noon.

Mr. White: Wow! You must have a lot of power lunches.

....

Moe: I saw a ghost in the school cafeteria.

Joe: Wow! Talk about a food fright.

....

Principal: Take a bite of this dessert. It'll perk you right up.

Teacher: What is it?

Principal: Coffee cake.

What do you get when a
cow eats lemons?

Bittermilk and sour cream.

....

What does a noisy ghost
like on a bagel?

Scream cheese.

....

What kind of bread do you get when
you cross lemons with a banker?

Sourdough bread.

....

What does the Little Mermaid
eat for dessert?

Fish cakes.

Lunchroom
Roll Call

U.R. Hungry

I.M. Starving

Al B. Late

Etta Snack

Stan N. Line

Harry Upp

Jimmy Foodfast

Opie Likesdis

Cole Drink

Mack Aroney

Frank Furter

Pete Zah

What do cows play at the lunch table?

Moosical chairs.

....

What do you call little frankfurters?

Tot dogs.

....

Cook: I got in a fight with a pot of gravy.

Lunch lady: So, what happened?

Cook: I gave it some lumps.

....

Why did all the little fishes stop swimming and open tiny brown bags?

It was time for their school lunch.

Kip: After I finished my dessert,
I belched ten times.

Rip: Maybe you ate a burpday cake.

....

What does Mrs. Air Rifle
feed her infants for lunch?

B-B food.

....

Why did Gretel scrub her brother
with soap and water at noontime?

*Her mother told her to wash her
Hans before eating lunch.*

....

Why was the bubblegum so upset?

His boss chewed him out.

Lunch lady: I spilled some pie filling.

Cook: Wipe it up with a sponge cake.

....

Boy: I dropped my lunch tray and now I have nothing to eat.

Girl: It sounds as if you're going on a crash diet today.

....

Girl: There's green slimy stuff on my gelatin dessert.

Boy: Relax. That's just Jell-O mold.

....

What did Mr. Spud use to lace up his sneakers?

Shoestring potatoes.

Cook: How do you want your cake,
          Mr. Hockey Player?

Player: Extra icing, please.

....

Joe: I own a restaurant that serves
          roasted water fowl with
          deep-fried pastries.

Moe: What do you call the place?

Joe: Duck N' Doughnuts.

....

Joni: I make a living selling sandwiches
          out of a bamboo shack.

Toni: What's your best-selling item?

Joni: A hut pastrami sandwich.

....

Wiley: Would you like some road
          runner stew?

Kyley: No, thanks. I don't like
          fast food.

What did the ghost order for lunch?

The Boo Plate Special.

....

What does the Invisible Man
eat for lunch?

Clear broth!

....

Why did the deli owner hire
the mummy?

*The mummy was great at wrapping
sandwiches.*

....

Is the werewolf a fast eater?

Yes. He always wolfs down his lunch.

Teacher: Why isn't Dracula, Jr.
              in the cafeteria?

Lunch Aide: He went to the batroom.

....

What do you get when you cross
a calf with a pirate sword?

A veal cutlass.

....

What do you get when you cross
a pig with an ax?

A pork chopper.

....

What do you get when you cross
a rabbit with a poodle?

A hop dog.

What do you get when you cross
a cafeteria with a flock of birds?

A lunch tweet.

....

What do you get when you cross Italian
cheese with paste?

Mozzarella sticks.

....

What does a top like to eat?

Spin-ach salad.

....

What do you get when you cross
a bee hive with dairy cows?

Swarm milk.

What kind of sandwich can
you make with playing cards?

A double-decker.

••

Hal: Do you drink tea, Sailor?

Sailor: No, coffee, Mate.

••

Why did the frankfurter
go to Hollywood?

To try out for some hotdog roles.

••

Director: Would you like to play a
            hotdog in a commercial?

Actor: I'd relish the part.

What is Ronald McDonald's
favorite side dish?

Big Mac-aroni and cheese.

....

Knock! Knock!

Who's there?

Olive.

Olive who?

Olive having spaghetti for lunch.

....

What do you get when you cross
bubblegum with a *Star Wars* hero?

Chewybacca.

....

What is a golfer's favorite
breakfast club?

A waffle iron.

News Flash!

Golfers like to eat lunch at
a drive-through restaurant.

....

Mr. Knife: Are you trying to steal
               my lunch?

Mr. Spoon: Yes. Fork it over!

....

What do you do if you don't
like the color of your food?

Diet!

....

Principal: Why did you give up making
           steak for lunch?

Cook: The recipe was too tough
           to follow and I just couldn't
           cut it.

Teacher: We don't allow students to drink milk through small paper tubes.

Boy: Now, that's the last straw!

....

What do you need to make home-run pancakes?

A really good batter.

....

SILLY SIGN IN A MEAT MARKET:

We sell our "ground" beef dirt cheap!

Knock! Knock!

Who's there?

Lima beans.

Lima beans who?

Lima beans up in a row and
I'll eat them one at a time.

....

How does a fortune teller
like her steak cooked?

Medium.

....

What do you get when you cross
a barbarian with a frankfurter roll?

Attila the Bun.

What does Tweety Bird eat for dessert?

Chocolate chirp cookies.

....

What did the river say to the chef?

"Your meals make my mouth water."

....

Chad: My computer is a big eater.

Brad: What do you mean?

Chad: It takes mega-bites.

....

Why are spiders so healthy?

They eat a lot of bee vitamins.

Teacher: We're going to teach you
how to put bubbles in
soda pop.

Student: Oh boy! A fizz-ed class.

....

Show Time!

**Show me a canary dipped
in chocolate—and I'll show you
a sweet tweet!**

....

Principal: Why are you sneezing
so much?

Teacher: Ah-choo! I had pepper
steak for lunch.

Knock! Knock!

Who's there?

Diesel.

Diesel who?

Diesel taste better with
ketchup on them.

····································

Knock! Knock!

Who's there?

Inn.

Inn who?

Inn digestion.

····································

How did the pig get so chubby?

It ate a lot of between-squeal snacks.

Daffy
Definition

What do you call a basket of shrimp?

A microweave.

....

What is Elvis's favorite steak song?

"Love Meat Tender."

....

What song did Elvis sing
to the frankfurter?

"You Ain't Nothing But a Hotdog."

....

What song did Elvis sing
to the milkshake?

"I'm All Shook Up!"

Knock! Knock!

Who's there?

Doughnut.

Doughnut who?

Doughnut leave the lunchroom
until the bell rings.

· ·

What breed of dog do you find
in the school cafeteria?

The lunch boxer.

· ·

Who is the smallest spud?

The tater tot.

· ·

Ted: I heard the cafeteria food is
really bad.

Ned: That's just a lunchroomer.

What's black and white and
works just like milk?

A nun-dairy creamer.

....

Boy: Is your stomach mad?

Teacher: No.

Boy: Then why is it grumbling?

....

Knock! Knock!

Who's there?

Salad.

Salad who?

Salad gold jewelry is expensive.

Daffy Definition

What do you call a school cafeteria?

A filling station where kids get gas.

....

Sal: This new drink is a real knockout.

Hal: It's only fruit punch.

....

Knock! Knock!

Who's there?

Noodle.

Noodle who?

Noodle you think you are, pal?

News Flash!

The Green Giant likes to eat
ham-and-peas sandwiches.

....

Chef: Some light bulbs fell into
             my pot of stew.

Custodian: So, watts cooking?

....

What is the most popular TV show
on the Cooking Channel?

"Bagel Watch."

....

What did the cheese sandwich
say to the detective?

"Please don't grill me."

Knock! Knock!

Who's there?

Don't snack.

Don't snack who?

**Don't snack up behind me.
It makes me nervous.**

....

**Where does the golf team
eat its lunch?**

At the table with fore-legs.

....

Which side dish do cats like to eat?

Mice-a-Roni.

BITE-SIZE SMILES

Veggie #1:   Hey, dude! Are you cool as a cucumber?

Veggie #2:   No, man! I'm totally rad-ish.

•••

What does a dragon
eat to stay healthy?

Three squire meals a day.

•••

How did the baseball umpire
get dirt in his mouth?

He licked his plate at lunch.

Boy: I feel like a sandwich.

Girl: I always knew you were full of baloney.

....

Elf: Mr. Claus, what do you want your sandwich made on?

Santa: Ho-Ho-Ho wheat bread.

....

Knock! Knock!

Who's there?

Rice.

Rice who?

Rice you to the other side of the cafeteria.

What is a potato's favorite game show?

"Peel of Fortune."

....

Student: Every time I go into the cafeteria, the color drains from my cheeks.

Nurse: Don't worry, it's just a little lunch pale.

....

Rudy: How do you make a gopher sandwich?

Judy: Use hole wheat bread.

What did the school bully
say to the astronaut?

Give me your launch money.

....

Which cartoon movie is about
a dog in the cafeteria?

"Lunch Lady and the Tramp."

....

Mr. Pig: I just lost my job.

Mr. Steer: Now you're a canned ham.

Mr. Apple:	Why are those guys complaining so much?
Mr. Pear:	Pay no attention to them. They're just gripe fruits.

....

What's green and rings?

A bell pepper.

....

What does Attila like to have with his tea?

Milk and Hun-ey.

Student cook: How did I do on my
scrambled eggs test?

Teacher: Grade A.

....

Knock! Knock!

Who's there?

Ricotta.

Ricotta who?

Ricotta thief breaking into
the lunchroom.

....

Where do giant apes go to eat
hamburgers for lunch?

Burger King Kong's Restaurant.

What would you like for dessert?

"Marble cake,"
said the sculptor.

"Sponge cake,"
said the mop salesman.

"Cupcakes,"
said the golfer.

"Pound cake,"
said the drummer.

"Layer cake,"
said the egg farmer.

"Cherry pi (π),"
said the algebra teacher.

Math teacher: I'm on a lemon diet.

Gym teacher: So, how's it going?

Math teacher: I still overeat at lunch, but I'm getting bitter.

....

Knock! Knock!

Who's there?

Wendy.

Wendy who?

Wendy kettle whistles, make hot chocolate.

....

When does a river gurgle?

When it talks with its mouth full.

What kind of pizza do you want for lunch?

"*Mush-room*,"
said the dogsledder.

"*Extra! Extra cheese*,"
said the newsboy.

"*Garlic*,"
said the vampire hunter.

"*Ant-chovies*,"
said the aardvark.

"*Thin crust*,"
said the weight watcher.

What do you get when you cross
a hen with cake batter?

A layer cake.

....

Man: I made a lot of money selling
      clear soup.

Boy: Are you a millionaire?

Man: No, I'm a boullionaire.

....

When is the best time to feed a plant?

When its taste buds start to bloom.

....

Lenny: Why is your face red?

Jenny: I always blush after meals.

What combination meal is made up of
blue seafood and steak?

Smurf and turf.

....

Knock! Knock!

Who's there?

Turnip.

Turnip who?

Turnip the heat or the water
will never boil.

....

How do you make friends
with an astronaut?

Take him out to launch.